Seven

Leatrice Ynostrosa

Presentation by *BookLeaf Publishing*

Web: www.bookleafpub.com

E-mail: info@bookleafpub.com

ISBN: 9789358736953

First edition 2022

DEDICATION

To my children:

Chase those dreams and gobble them up bit by bit.

ACKNOWLEDGEMENT

I'd like to thank my children for inspiring these words and allowing me to be a better person by being their mother. I'd like to thank my husband for tolerating my antics and helping me when I fall. Finally, I'd like to thank Robin Alvarez for inspiring and encouraging me. Here is to sh***y first drafts!

PREFACE

I have seven precious children.

One is on the cusp on manhood. One is growing into herself as a person. One is stuck between childhood and teenage years. One is struggling with emotions far bigger than herself.

One is facing the biggest fight anyone must face: the fight against one's own body.

One was too small to be acknowledged by the world.

One was born too early and left before anyone was ready.

These are their poems.

Survivor

"I want Cinderella hair!"
The six year old demands.
So I start to work,
brushing gently upward,
swooping slippery blonde hair
into a tiny sloppy bun.
Secure with a pink scrunchie.
She prances to the mirror,
humming with approval.

Her older sister watches silently
and opens a squeaky drawer.
She chooses a headband
from the array of colors:
Sparkle and tinsel,
two bobbing stars.

She crowns her own head
Highlights the victory
of new, regrowing curls.
My seven-year-old survivor's
unspoken declaration—
"I'm a girl, too."

Raw

I cried at my desk, looking at an email with blue
confetti and "Congrats it's a boy."
Despite our fear and shock of your sudden
existence,
We knew you'd be fine because you were a gift
from God.
My thoughts of "I'm too old for this (at the
tender age of 35)"
Were tempered with the dizzying ideas of
cuddling a swaddled newborn in my arms.
I cautiously prepared for you, buying tiny
onesies and miniature moccasins,
resisting the urge to buy every baby item before
your shower.
Even when the doctor said you had passed,
When she showed your now still heart and gave
her condolences,
I didn't believe her because God has asked us to
trust and we did.
Why would he pull you away from me weeks
after the danger had passed?
I prayed for a miracle as I lay waiting for
surgery,
Thinking she'd open me up and you'd be there,
kicking and squirming.

Instead, you died sucking your thumb, peacefully,
And were delivered to me in a hand crocheted cocoon
That another mother who had gone through hell had made.
I held you to the breast you'd never suckle, next to my heart.
I sang you the lullabies I've sang all my babies, knowing you could hear from heaven.
I prayed thanks for being able to hold you,
As I was never able to hold your brother before (I asked him to watch over you).
Two days later, I laid you in a tiny cooler for your long trip to the funeral home.
Unable to watch them place the lid over your tiny frame,
I instead lost myself to darkness in your grandmother's arms,
Unable to believe I'd never see you or hold you again.
You were buried in the cemetery where your great grandparents are,
Next to other little lost babies and a set of twins,
In a cocoon and blanket your Dad and I crocheted through tears,
 So that we could give you something before you left (I kept the original one).

You were lowered in the earth lying a tiny casket
your grandpa worked days on;
there were sunflowers over your grave and a
statue of Jesus with the children nearby.
And that was the end. There are no more
pictures beyond the few I took in those two
days.
There are no more memories to build, even now
when I am still supposed to be pregnant.
There are finite bits of you near me, your
footprints the size of my fingernail,
The blanket they placed under you rolled up on
my bed (It still smells like you),
The hole in my soul with the ragged edges
where your life was ripped from me.
I cried at my desk today, burning tears of
torment as I think about you.

Glimpses

5

Towering gentle giant
Suppresses fears and emotions.
Quiet and contained,
Like magma under the earth's crust.
Disillusioned so young:
With the world,
With childhood.
Jaded and knowledgeable,
A child who spoken to angels
And prophesied siblings.
My first exploration into motherhood,
My first mistakes and triumphs realized,
Toddler cuddles have become awkward hugs,
Gawky arms draped over shoulders.
Almost a man and yet not rushing to leave,
On the cusp of his potential.

Discus

Two feet grip for purchase
In men's size twelve sneakers
Air is blown through lips
Full and lush and lipstick free
Muscled shoulders roll
Delicate neck twists side to side
To release nervous tension and focus
Curls frame her face
Green eyes focus far down the field
One twist of the torso
Arms outstretched
Two twists of the torso
Muscles memorized the move
A third twist and the spin starts
One full rotation
Arm whips around
Clean release
The discus flies forward gracefully
Victory is in her eyes

Heritage

My children have been cheated

by a world that won't fully recognize them,

beautiful blonde strangers

who have more understanding of quinceañeras

than of sweet sixteens.

Society says they are privileged,

while their last name still holds them back

in everything but affirmative action.

They know so much of Mexican matanzas

and so little of block parties.

Their pale skin marks them racist;

they can't relate to color

(cousins with skin from latte to espresso).

They dance cumbias and polkas

and stumble in their waltzes.

I weep for my children, stuck between races.

My husband's blood gives them a family

that extends like supporting tree branches.

My blood marks them with suspicion,

born of their blue eyes.

An Angel Came Wearily

An angel came wearily, heart full of stone
To pick up a burden that cut to the bone.
Her mission was not to ponder God's will
But to simply obey and His wish to fulfill.
The angel knelt silently by a mother unknowing
And studied the life that inside her was growing.
The babe wanted to stay, as every child does
Safe with his mother, surrounded by love.
She spoke to his soul, calming his fear:
God wanted him home and needed him near.
With the only sadness he would ever know
The babe left his parents and the world below.
Now safe in the warmth of Jesus's strong arms
The sweet babe is free from all hurt and all
harm.
Down on Earth, the parents don't feel the same:
They are struck down by grief, bitterness, and
pain.
Knowing that one day they will see their dear
child
Allows them to walk their path mile by long
mile.
Tomorrow, a new babe the angel will greet,
And build God's kingdom by two tiny feet.

Kraken

Little perfect doll: blue eyes, blonde hair
Perfection to sooth an aching mother
Tiny frame belying the fire within
Thunder, toughness, stubbornness
Your first words? "Don't touch me!"
Quickly followed by, "Cuz I want to."
Fierce competitor in sports
Sweet face hiding your hidden beast
Stealing balls and shooting goals with ease
Pain is temporary in your mind
A single "ow" your only response
Now your strength is tested
Gone is baby you were promised to hold
You talk to him, your missing brother
Your dolls all have his name
One so small should never have to process
The loss of a sibling without notice
But that's God's doing, not my own
Your days are filled with the exuberance of
youth
Your nights are filled holding a shadow

Pieces of Mercy

Her body proclaims her strength:
Muscular thighs, broad hands.
She flips tractor tires with ease.

A pebble puppy turned rockhound,
Who tumbles agate and collects gems-
Each piece a memory made in stone.

She paints scenes of peaceful places,
Of stormy sunsets and mystic moonrises
And always, fields of bright sunflowers.

She works hard at everything life,
Fighting dyslexia, ADD, and bullies,
Earning every inch with sweat.

She dances unabashedly,
Her body moving without thought
Lost to the songs and rhythm within.

She loves wholeheartedly,
Her friends, her pets, her family,
Even the brother who doesn't like her.

Cusp

You are firmly in the middle of things-
Of the siblings, of adolescence, of other's
business-
You are comfortable there in the middle.
Observant above all, as you have always been.
Once a small babe with concentration on your
face,
Trying to understand the world you were thrust
in
Now instigating events and watching the
outcomes.
Sill drawn to the unencumbered joys of
childhood,
Of make believe, of magic, and of innocence.
Wanting those hugs and kisses of boyhood.
Yet you push forward excitedly into puberty,
Flattering girls and their fearsome fathers
With smooth spoken lines and dancing hips.
The man you will be is not yet formed
But he shines in tiny bits from your hazel eyes
The unhurried way you move across a room,
The confident tilt of your shoulders,
A mirror of your father and grandfather.
The charming smile and dusting of freckles

Underneath a nest of red rambunctious hair:
Proof that you are not as content as you seem,
That you must move life to suit yourself.
A young man, Mama's baby, a hidden trickster
On the cusp of discovering your way in life.

Pain

It's an integral part of motherhood-

Physical pain in birthing,
Tearing your flesh to release your babe,
Bleeding nipples chapped
At the hungry maws of tiny humans,
Sore noses, foreheads, crotches
At the overzealous love of toddlers.

There's the anguish of mental pain,
Forgotten months of infancy,
Clouded by the haze of darkness
Depression that can swallow you,
Stealing memories that now are only in photos.
Not just after birth but before-
Desperately writing farewell letters
As your babe squirms in protest inside you,
Hating that you don't want to exist
And hiding it from everyone you love.

But the worst is the emotional pain,
When you must hold down tiny arms
And ignore the screams of fear again,
So doctors can stab with shiny needles,
Plunging poison into tiny veins:

Injuring them to save their life.
When your child went where you can't follow
Empty arms, grieving heart, shattered soul.
When you recognize those emotions
In your other children's eyes
You reach out and hold them tightly
like you wish you could hold their sibling
But you know you can't soothe
That familiar ache in their souls.

400 Meter Dash

READY!
Feet find purchase on the block
A false start to test
Reset and breathe.

SET!
Legs straighten
Hands brace
Deep breath in.

BANG!
Adrenaline fuels the first few meters
Joy in movement the next fifty.
Strong legs surging
Rhythmic slapping feet
The urge to pass the man in front.
Around the final turn,
Now plunging into his reserves.
As he draws nearer to the lead,
Manic screams from the stands:
Calling his name, telling him to push.
Heart throbbing, lungs empty,
Final lean across the finish line
Breathless, hands on knees
Cramps accompany victory.

One Day at a Time

One day you were born screaming at the world.

One day you woke with a lump in your neck
And we discovered our lives would change.

One day you sat on your bed, scowling,
Crying because you'd forgotten how to subtract;
Your mind refused to bring the knowledge to
you.

One day you rode your tricycle down the hall
Slowly, as fast as you could manage.
You held up your orange bucket,
And asked the nurse, "trick or treat?"

One day you barely woke up:
Your body was so tired and worn,
A shade of the healthy girl you were.
The nurse made you a sparkling holder
For the tooth you lost that night.

One day you packed up your hospital room,
Took down all your paintings,
Placed crafting supplies in little baskets.
You tied red three balloons to your backpack

And chatted with the nurses
As Mom stuffed the car to the brim.

One day you ran down the court
Slower than the others, but chasing still.
You passed the ball to teammates
And jumped in excitement at a basket.
You wore your hair in two buns
And no one asked about your scar,
Proof of the battle you are winning.

The Significance of Numbers

1 test joyfully revealing you
Celebrating you
Proof you were here

9 days of knowing you,
Loving you,
Praying you would stay

9 days of numbing fear
Every twinge
Every tiny crimson drop

1 test; a single line
You'd gone
 My heart fell shattered

9 years of remembering
July 2012
Grieving that dark day

A lifetime of missing you
My hidden fourth child
The one I don't speak of
Hating myself for my inability to keep you

Wild Child

She's never met an animal she doesn't like.
Last year she had daily pet cicadas
Their buzzing made her squeal with joy.
She cried when her tiny pet snake
Disappeared from its cage overnight;
She asked if she could have brother's.
Undeterred by scales or slime,
She proudly poses with lizards
And the giant salamander
Who hides in the pond
Where her ducklings swim.
Those four tiny fluffs follow her around.
She tackled the neighbor's new dog
 Who sniffed to close to her ducks;
She's too little to do much
But hold the half-grown pup still
While adults come to the rescue.
Every tadpole and toad are hers,
Every chicken bows to her reach.
My tiniest child braving the wild
With love, kisses, and dirty hands.

High School Gauntlet

You hate high school because, like every girl
ever born
You are buffeted by the wind of hate born of
anger.
You're too loud, too kind, too ugly; you care too
much.
What those other kids break you down for
Is exactly what you must preserve at all costs.
Your loud, flamboyant nature is a precious
commodity!
You stand up for yourself, for what is right,
You are passionate in all you do.
Do not let others curb your happiness
To suit their miserable minds.
Your kindness is your best quality:
You care deeply for others,
Particularly the outcasts and the wronged.
Like mother Theresa, you want to draw them to
you;
May you continue to see Jesus in every person.
Your beauty is hidden from you
Stolen by cruel comments over miniscule things.
Your smile is stunning and other hate it
Because they have forgotten how to smile:
With their whole being, without restraint.

Your physical strength is intimidating
Because it is a mirror of your interior strength,
And those broken fear strength they've lost.
Never stop being your authentic self,
Yours is the soul that makes the world
uncomfortable
Because it reminds them of what they have
given up.
Make them squirm and show them what they are
missing.

In His Blood

Vision is limited by his helmet,
The sweat dripping in his eyes.
He gnaws on his mouthguard,
His face a threat to his opponent.
HIKE!
Down his shoulders dip
Followed by the surge upward,
Entire bodyweight behind the effort;
Lifting and pushing,
The other boy slams to the ground.
Our player quickly resets,
Scans for the ball and more enemies-
Ready to conquer the field.
A shrill whistle blow signals
The release of his fury.
The predator becomes once again
A smiling 11-year-old boy.

Jimmy's Lullaby

You are my sunshine, my only sunshine
I used to revel in the secret knowledge of you,
Tucked safe under my heart, a tiny dancer.
I knew you were a boy before the tests told me
so

You make me happy when skies are grey
Your siblings delighted in your existence,
Not wanting to grow and leave you alone,
But eager to help rock you, change you, love
you.

You'll never know dear how much I love you
Praying that day that you were being stubborn,
Hiding from me like you did so often,
Staring stunned at the black and white screen;
Where a flutter should be, only stillness reigned.

Please don't take my sunshine away
Holding you the next day in my hands,
So tiny, so perfect, ten little fingers and toes.
Softly rocking you and singing you lullabies
Saying hello, my son, as I was saying goodbye.

Snippets

Watching her, I see still life photos
Of times that have happened before.
A tiny baby, happy in her swing,
Dad's yellow blanket up to her chin,
A pacifier hanging out of her mouth.
A goofy pigtailed toddler
Hanging upside down from the couch,
Munching an apple and watching TV.
A tanned little girl in a swimsuit
Smiling gap-toothed at her very first fish,
But refusing to touch it for pictures.
A tired smiling girl
Posing for a photo with her coloring project,
Her IV the only evidence of disease.
A sick little girl struggling
With a pink birthday boa around her neck
And a bedazzled eyepatch to cover her wound.
A sleeping little girl
No hair, every bone visible
Waking only to smile at the therapy dog.
A bald little girl smiling
Pedaling furiously down the hall on her trike,
Dad flying behind pushing her IV pole.
A strong little girl
Regrowing hair dyed purple
Laughing while I take her picture.

Inheritance

You get your luck from me
And in part, your red hair
Your freckles are mine,
As is tripping on air.

You get your moves from dad
Your ease with girls
Your troublesome smile
Your dances and whirls.

But your need to be naughty
To stir the pot with a spoon
Your need to joke around
Son, that's all YOU.

Big Talk

Beautiful smile
Irresistible dimple
Crooked abs
Teenage heartthrob
Built to run
Tall and thin
Too intelligent
Over thinks
Gentle heart
Feels deeply
Mother's son
Father's sidekick
Almost adult
Junior year
World ahead
Ambitions established
His only wish:
To fish.

Beatific Vision

Two boys walk hand in hand
Barefoot down the dusty road.
There must be a frog in a pocket,
Fishing poles over shoulders,
Laughter easy on their lips.
They look like each other,
These sweet little boys.
They have my dimple,
Their daddy's big smile.
Perhaps one is a redhead,
And the other must be blonde.
They have to be naughty
In the innocent way of youth:
Maybe stealing haloes
Or dumping rainbows on clear days.
Every Sunday they sit together,
The grieving family and their boys.
For an hour they mingle
Their deep love and their sorrow.
Afterwards, the boys run out to play,
Chasing fireflies in the dusk.
Their great grandparents watch,
Or joyfully join in the hunt.
Often, they all stop and are still,
Seeing their family below.

Then they pray for the parents
With too empty arms and hopeful hearts.